G000296011

This Journal Belongs to:

_____

Spiritual
Journal
for Women

Mindfulness, Gratitude, and Meditation Prompts to Reconnect with You

LEAH GUY

ROCKRIDGE
PRESS

Copyright © 2021 by Rockridge Press, Emeryville, California

No part of this publication may be reproduced, stored in a retrieval system, or transmitted in any form or by any means, electronic, mechanical, photocopying, recording, scanning, or otherwise, except as permitted under Sections 107 or 108 of the 1976 United States Copyright Act, without the prior written permission of the Publisher. Requests to the Publisher for permission should be addressed to the Permissions Department, Rockridge Press 6005 Shellmound Street, Suite 175, Emeryville, CA 94608.

Limit of Liability/Disclaimer of Warranty: The Publisher and the author make no representations or warranties with respect to the accuracy or completeness of the contents of this work and specifically disclaim all warranties, including without limitation warranties of fitness for a particular purpose. No warranty may be created or extended by sales or promotional materials. The advice and strategies contained herein may not be suitable for every situation. This work is sold with the understanding that the Publisher is not engaged in rendering medical, legal, or other professional advice or services. If professional assistance is required, the services of a competent professional person should be sought. Neither the Publisher nor the author shall be liable for damages arising herefrom. The fact that an individual, organization, or website is referred to in this work as a citation and/or potential source of further information does not mean that the author or the Publisher endorses the information the individual, organization, or website may provide or recommendations they/it may make. Further, readers should be aware that websites listed in this work may have changed or disappeared between when this work was written and when it is read.

For general information on our other products and services or to obtain technical support, please contact our Customer Care Department within the United States at (866) 744-2665, or outside the United States at (510) 253-0500.

Rockridge Press publishes its books in a variety of electronic and print formats. Some content that appears in print may not be available in electronic books, and vice versa.

TRADEMARKS: Rockridge Press and the Rockridge Press logo are trademarks or registered trademarks of Callisto Media Inc. and/or its affiliates, in the United States and other countries, and may not be used without written permission. All other trademarks are the property of their respective owners. Rockridge Press is not associated with any product or vendor mentioned in this book.

Interior and Cover Designer: Francesca Pacchini
Art Producer: Janice Ackerman
Editor: Lia Ottaviano
Production Editor: Emily Sheehan
Cover & Interior Illustration: Courtesy of Creative Market
Author Photo: Courtesy of Barry Morganstein Photography

ISBN: Print 978-1-64876-610-7
R0

*To my grandmother Grace Ludema Guy,
who was a loving angel on Earth and continues
to guide me from above.*

Contents

"The personal life deeply lived always expands into truths beyond itself."

—Anaïs Nin

Introduction

Welcome to your spiritual journal. This is a place for you to reflect, share, and reconnect with your highest self, by gaining new insights or remembering those of old. Journaling is an effective tool for self-care and personal growth, offering a meditative quality while inviting you to pause and connect to the sacred space within. I encourage you to use this journal daily, or as often as you feel inspired, and follow the prompts as closely as possible. They will assist you on your spiritual path, guiding you to find ease in your life and in the world.

Here, you will gain connection to your true self, and experience an opportunity to dive deep within and uncover the most authentic version of you. As you begin to live more authentically, you will begin to experience peace, happiness, and love. As with most practices, the more you do the work, the more the work will work.

This journal uses prompts, meditations, mantras, and powerful quotes based in mindfulness, yogic traditions, and positive psychology to expand your consciousness, encourage self-acceptance, and free us from the insecurity, fear, and self-doubt that can limit our lives. This book offers spirituality for everyone, from beginners to advanced practitioners, regardless of affiliation.

Each part of the book is a different tool. The prompts offer something to reflect on in writing, while the practices invite you to reflect as you go about your daily life. Mantras are phrases to guide you into a place of self-reflection and can be used in meditation or as simple reminders throughout the day. They help bring you back to the moment and your inner self. You may like to write out the mantras and post them on your mirror, bedside table, or on the office computer. The meditations in this journal can be practiced at any time and in any location. Whenever you have a few moments or need to reset, allow yourself the gift of meditation. I advise you to first read through the meditations and practice them in line with the journal entries. If you find one that particularly resonates, you can record it into a device or jot down the key points to use as reminders during your day. Meditation practice can be as short as pausing to notice a breath or as long as you are able to participate. There is no right or best way to meditate; however, a consistent practice will yield the most positive effect.

Over two decades of professional training in energy healing, mindfulness, and spirituality, along with a lifetime spent overcoming trauma, eating disorders, and anxiety, led me on the path to my own healing and to the approach I use in my work. I am a testament to the fact that we each have the ability to transform pain and rise up to meet our higher selves. Part of this process is looking closely at what resonates with your heart and soul. The more you align with your soul, the more freedom and ease you embody.

Writing a spiritual journal for women resonates with my belief that we all need support and an ongoing practice to live a life that is meaningful, successful, and fulfilling. I became interested in spirituality at a young age, developing practices of prayer, intuition, and communication with angels and light workers. In my alone time, I craved connection to something bigger than myself as a way to learn how to self-soothe and cope. My relationship with spirituality has been an anchor in my life, centering me in the truth of who I am—a divine being full of worth and purpose having an amazing human experience.

Journaling has always been part of my journey. My journal is a compassionate partner, a safe place to share feelings, thoughts, and emotions that may be too difficult to discuss with other people. When we journal without the filter of judgment, we can work through the limitations of the mind and inner conflict. I've learned that as I become freer to share my thoughts and feelings in a journal, I gain the capacity to extend more compassion and empathy to others.

In this journal, you will start by getting to know yourself more deeply, then move through different themes of spirituality that will bring you closer to your highest self. Please note that while a guided journal practice is a great way to work through any challenging feelings and emotions, this book is not a replacement for a therapist, medication, or medical treatment. There is no shame in seeking whatever help we may need.

How you identify yourself is important in your spiritual growth. Your identity up until now may be connected to labels put on you by society, family, or friends. Although those labels may describe who you are in relation to others, you are so much more than that. You are a beautiful, strong, and unique being meant to be here just as you are. The world needs exactly what you have to offer. When self-doubt arises, open your heart to acknowledge the innocent soul who emerged in this world full of life, vibrant, and personality, brimming with purpose.

You may forge your own path but with the presence of love and the support of your soul tribe you will never walk alone. I hope you enjoy this guided journal experience, opening up to new possibilities, finding comfort in your being, and reconnecting with the true essence of who you really are.

Peace be with you.

Chapter One

Connect to Your Core

One of the first steps to living a spiritual life is connecting to your core. Living authentically requires a deeper look at your heart, mind, and passions. You may stumble across aspects of yourself that are difficult to accept, but when you do, keep going; self-acceptance is a soothing ointment that softens resistance to insecurities and fear.

Spiritual growth asks you to move through fear and insecurities and make choices that resonate with your true self. You no longer seek approval, as approval comes from within. Authentic living is not only freeing; it allows you to act on what inspires you, brings joy, and allows a rich and rewarding life.

Inner child work and exploration are great ways to start connecting to your passions and purpose. Your inner child is pure light, a gift to the world, and has so much more to say. As you deepen your connection to your self, the path to your purpose becomes clearer.

"Put it down in capital letters: SELF-DEVELOPMENT IS A HIGHER DUTY THAN SELF-SACRIFICE."

—Elizabeth Cady Stanton

How others perceive us is often different from how we see ourselves. What might your family members say if they were describing you to their friends? And how would your friends describe you?

_____

_____

_____

_____

_____

_____

_____

_____

_____

_____

_____

_____

_____

_____

_____

_____

PRACTICE

Looking back over the last 20 years, how have you

changed and developed as a person? How have you

fostered your creative life and enriched your spiritual life?

Think about the last time you felt pulled to choose something that was out of the norm. Did you follow your desire and do it? Why or why not? Looking back, how do you feel about that decision now? Choosing different foods, apparel, or even artistic expressions can add adventure and diversity in your life.

_____

_____

_____

_____

_____

_____

_____

_____

_____

_____

_____

_____

_____

_____

_____

_____

_____

_____

_____

When you think about your upbringing, what was the story of your childhood? Write out the names of the main characters, the costars, and the supporting players. What was a storyline that was repetitive in your life or impactful to you as a child?

_____

_____

_____

_____

_____

_____

_____

_____

_____

_____

_____

_____

_____

_____

_____

_____

I am exactly
who I am meant to be.

Imagine yourself as a small child. Who was that beautiful soul? Recall some of your favorite dolls or toys and the shows or games you loved. Maybe you remember a certain hairstyle, outfit, or favorite pair of shoes. What were some of your favorite activities when alone or with others?

_____

_____

_____

_____

_____

_____

_____

_____

_____

_____

_____

_____

_____

_____

_____

_____

_____

_____

MEDITATION

Get comfortable and relaxed. Allow your eyes to soften and become aware of your breath. Now imagine yourself as a child, between the ages of four and eight years old. Notice her hair, her smile, and any other details that you can remember. Allow that child to take you to her room or an outdoor space where she often spent time. Just observe her. Notice her actions, her facial expressions, the lightness or heaviness of her heart. Breathe in love and appreciation for her. Spend as much time here with her as you like. When you are ready, return the focus to your breath, to your body, and to being present in your current space.

While witnessing your inner child, what emotions did you feel in your body? What emotions did you sense her feeling? How are they different or the same?

_____

_____

_____

_____

_____

_____

_____

_____

_____

_____

_____

_____

_____

_____

_____

_____

_____

Tuning into your inner child, imagine what she may need that she didn't fully receive. Does she need more playtime or laughter? More attention, encouragement, or snuggles? Think of ways you can offer her more nurturing so her spirit can feel safe and loved. Write a list of three things you want her to have and explain why you want her to have them.

_____

_____

_____

_____

_____

_____

_____

_____

_____

_____

_____

_____

_____

_____

_____

_____

_____

_____

As a young person, were you smart or sassy, creative or a great thinker? Did you have the heart to heal people, or a special bond with nature or animals? What characteristics did you have as a young girl?

_____

_____

_____

_____

_____

_____

_____

_____

_____

_____

_____

_____

_____

_____

_____

_____

_____

_____

_____

_____

"We already have everything we need. There is no need for self-improvement ... all the time our warmth and brilliance are right here. This is who we really are. We are one blink of an eye away from being fully awake."

—Pema Chödrön

PRACTICE

In your bedroom or meditation space, create an altar for your inner child. Include a picture of yourself at a young age, along with some things you loved back then. Add in crystals, a live plant, and inspired art that speaks to your heart.

We often hold ourselves back or abandon our desires for fear that we will not have the approval of others. The voice that stirs in your soul is asking to be heard. What is she saying?

_____

_____

_____

_____

_____

_____

_____

_____

_____

_____

_____

_____

_____

_____

_____

_____

_____

_____

MEDITATION

Focus on your breath as it comes in through the nose. Imagine that you can take the breath all the way through your body. Breathing in, your energy lightens as it connects up and out through the crown of your head. Breathing out, your body becomes settled in the grounded connection through your feet.

Without deepening the breath, deepen your focus. As you inhale, notice the expansion of your energy field. As you exhale, integrate that expanded energy sensation into your body and relax even more. Continue for a few moments, then bring your awareness back to your body and open your eyes.

Notice your energy in different locations. You may feel comfortable at a friend's home but not as peaceful at your sister's place. What is the difference? Notice how you feel in your own bedroom, compared to when you are outdoors in a garden. Consider things that make you feel joyful and peaceful. How can you bring elements of those things into your personal space? Write about them below.

_____

_____

_____

_____

_____

_____

_____

_____

_____

_____

_____

_____

_____

_____

_____

_____

Do you struggle with the fear of not knowing? What does that fear look like? Where do you feel it in your body? As if you were offering advice to a friend, write down a few ways you could give yourself permission to not know and continue moving forward anyway.

_____

_____

_____

_____

_____

_____

_____

_____

_____

_____

_____

_____

_____

_____

_____

_____

_____

Do you catch yourself having fearful thoughts, limited beliefs, or insecurities about your worth or abilities? Write three of those thoughts or beliefs down. Now look them over. Are they true, or are they someone else's beliefs? Write the answer below each thought or belief.

_____

_____

_____

_____

_____

_____

_____

_____

_____

_____

_____

_____

_____

_____

_____

_____

_____

_____

Trusting in something larger than yourself can bring not only peace of mind but excitement to discover what is in store for your life. Think of situations in your life right now where you feel out of control. Why do you feel like you need to control these situations? What would happen if instead you relaxed your grip and received what is being offered to you now? Write about what that might look like.

_____

_____

_____

_____

_____

_____

_____

_____

_____

_____

_____

_____

_____

_____

What have you been resisting lately? Tense feelings, triggers, and old wounds can cause us to avoid trying new things or stepping into the unknown. Write down three things that you have been resisting. They can be anything from looking for a new job to dealing with a cluttered area of your home. How could you take one courageous step toward acceptance here?

_____

_____

_____

_____

_____

_____

_____

_____

_____

_____

_____

_____

_____

_____

_____

_____

_____

_____

Staying in the now prevents your mind and energy from drifting into your past stories or future anxieties. Bring all of your awareness to this very moment. Are you safe right now? How does this moment feel?

_____

_____

_____

_____

_____

_____

_____

_____

_____

_____

_____

_____

_____

_____

_____

_____

_____

"The beginning is always today."

—Mary Wollstonecraft Shelley

When was the last time you allowed yourself to play and be creative? Make a plan to find time in the next week to let yourself create, laugh, rest, play, and be free. Plan for at least three times when you can devote a minimum of 10 to 15 minutes to this.

_____

_____

_____

_____

_____

_____

_____

_____

_____

_____

_____

_____

_____

_____

_____

_____

_____

PRACTICE

Gift yourself the time, money, and energy you need to discover one passion that you might have neglected or been afraid to try. What makes your heart sing? What makes you excited to start the day? Do that.

MEDITATION

This is a walking meditation you can practice either in nature or while strolling through town. Before leaving, set an intention to "see" and "feel" the world differently. Don't bring any bags or noisy keys.

If in nature, allow your eyes to be soft, gazing forward and taking in the colors, textures, and smells of the earth. Be slow, mindful, and in receipt of what you observe. If walking in town, move even slower, allowing space for your mind and body to take in the multitude of sights and sounds. Imagine becoming one with the environment, offering beams of light and healing vibrations out to your community as you walk.

Sometimes change feels scary and uncomfortable. We fear the unknown and get used to our own expectations. What fears have kept you from coming out of your comfort zone?

_____

_____

_____

_____

_____

_____

_____

_____

_____

_____

_____

_____

_____

_____

_____

_____

_____

_____

Creativity is the expression of one's soul. How can you express yourself today in words, art, music, food, design, organization, or intimacy?

_____

_____

_____

_____

_____

_____

_____

_____

_____

_____

_____

_____

_____

_____

_____

_____

How do you identify yourself? Without using words that connect you to others (mom, sister, wife, friend) or a job title, write a couple of sentences that describe who you are. Let your expression be colorful to capture your essence!

_____

_____

_____

_____

_____

_____

_____

_____

_____

_____

_____

_____

_____

_____

_____

_____

PRACTICE

Create a vision board for your life. Use magazine
pictures or personal drawings to illustrate the things you
want to invite into your life, as well as the joys that are
already present. Paste the images on the board and let the
visual feed your soul and the dreams you want to fulfill.
When finished, hang the board in an area of your
home where you often spend time. This way it will be a
constant reminder.

Life is working for me, not against me.

Trusting that the universe has your back isn't always easy. Remember that divine timing is real, there are no accidents or coincidences, and you can choose to respond from your highest self. What are three situations that you are worried about right now? Identify a way you can work to trust the universe in each situation.

_____

_____

_____

_____

_____

_____

_____

_____

_____

_____

_____

_____

_____

_____

_____

_____

There's no judgment on the value of your purpose. Your contribution is as impactful as anyone else's—the world needs what you have to offer. Our lives have an impact on the world; however, we often don't see it. The smallest act from the heart can save a life. What is your heart offering today?

Chapter Two
Grow with Gratitude

When we deepen our relationship with gratitude, we enrich our spiritual lives. Gratitude is not just being thankful; it is a readiness to show appreciation and kindness as well. Gratitude is the potion that brings magic to the mundane. Cultivating an intentional practice of gratitude can open our hearts and expand our souls. To feel gratitude, we must practice presence, awareness, and acceptance.

A practice of gratitude leads to less stress, better relationships, and a greater ability to handle change. Gratitude steers our focus away from what's wrong and onto what's right. We redirect our focus from anxieties about the things that have not yet blossomed to appreciation of things that are in full bloom. Viewing your world through a lens of gratitude, you will experience more peace, more contentment, and more fulfillment.

What are you grateful for? Start listing as many things as you can think of without filtering yourself. See if you can fill an entire page with loving thoughts of appreciation.

_____

_____

_____

_____

_____

_____

_____

_____

_____

_____

_____

_____

_____

_____

_____

_____

_____

_____

PRACTICE

Finding gratitude in a situation that seems difficult can help alleviate mental or emotional stress. Which situation feels like a burden to you? Perhaps it's having to rise early for work or frequently reminding your spouse to do chores. Can you practice finding gratitude for the opportunity to work or for the commitment of your relationship in order to shift your energy into a more positive state?

What has someone done for you that you'd like to pay forward?

_____

_____

_____

_____

_____

_____

_____

_____

_____

_____

_____

_____

_____

_____

_____

_____

_____

_____

_____

Feeling appreciation for others can help you to reap huge rewards in your heart. You can appreciate anyone who touches your life in any way—local farmers who produce your favorite foods, street vendors who put out elegant flower arrangements each day, small business owners who beautify your town, or neighbors who keep their sidewalk clean. Who comes to mind for you?

I am thankful for all that I am,
for all that I have.

Gratitude for food sources adds a dimension to our meals, as well as our hearts. Buying foods locally, or growing your own, helps you become more aware of the foods that nourish you and all it takes for them to grow: planting, watering, tending, and harvesting. How can you find appreciation for the foods that keep you alive and healthy?

_____

_____

_____

_____

_____

_____

_____

_____

_____

_____

_____

_____

_____

_____

_____

_____

MEDITATION

For this meditation, allow yourself the luxury of rest. Get comfortable and recline on a bed or sofa. Close your eyes and imagine sitting in front of a beautiful sturdy tree with buds about to blossom. Bring to mind things and people for which you are grateful. Imagine writing one of these things on a large green leaf and hanging it on the tree. Each person or thing you think of gets its own leaf. One by one, write them on the leaves and attach each one to a tree branch. Continue until the beautiful tree is full of leaves. Relax and allow the tree to reflect all of the riches in your life.

Appreciating the people in your life is wonderful, but relaying that gratitude opens their hearts as well. What small act of kindness can you offer to your neighbor, mail carrier, or colleague this week to show them you are grateful?

_____

_____

_____

_____

_____

_____

_____

_____

_____

_____

_____

_____

_____

_____

_____

We all have to-do lists in our minds each day. We may forget that caring for things and people comes from a place of love. List a few of your responsibilities and how they are coming from a place of love.

_____

_____

_____

_____

_____

_____

_____

_____

_____

_____

_____

_____

_____

_____

_____

_____

Plants and gardens bring many benefits into our lives. What plant do you feel especially grateful for? Write a thank-you note to that plant below, sharing gratitude for its ability to keep the air healthy or for its nutritional value.

_____

_____

_____

_____

_____

_____

_____

_____

_____

_____

_____

_____

_____

_____

Think of something that brings you awe. Why do you feel awed by it? What other feelings does it stir up? Is there a way you can incorporate those feelings into your daily life a bit more?

_____

_____

_____

_____

_____

_____

_____

_____

_____

_____

_____

_____

_____

_____

_____

PRACTICE

Create a gratitude jar. Every day, write something you're

grateful for on a slip of paper and drop it into the jar.

At the end of the month, empty the jar and reread the

comments to recount your blessings.

MEDITATION

Still your body and quiet your mind. With eyes open in a soft gaze, focus on your breath. Place your right hand on your chest, then put your left hand on top of your right. Follow the breath as it travels into your lungs, expanding and fueling the body with life. Feel the gratitude well up in your chest. As it does, see if you can connect to the beating of your heart. These two organs are working so diligently to support your being, allowing you to experience another moment of life, breath by breath. Send these organs loving appreciation for their tireless work.

Spend some time with your favorite songs. What about the music and lyrics touches your soul? Write a thank-you letter to those musicians, expressing your gratitude for the immense level of talent, skill, and work that went into making that music. Offer the musicians your gratitude by receiving their work with appreciation, dancing, singing, and enjoyment. You don't have to send the note to the musicians (unless you want to!).

Make a list of three or four people who have impacted your life. These could be teachers, lovers, friends, or just a stranger who was kind to you. Write a short sentence of appreciation to each person, letting them know how meaningful they were in your life.

_____

_____

_____

_____

_____

_____

_____

_____

_____

_____

_____

_____

_____

_____

_____

_____

Using your senses, become mindful of the everyday sounds, smells, and sights that are in your life. Take a moment to pause and intentionally experience each of these. What did it feel like to use each sense? Write about what you smelled, what you heard, what you felt, or what you saw.

_____

_____

_____

_____

_____

_____

_____

_____

_____

_____

_____

_____

_____

_____

_____

_____

"One's life has value so long as one attributes value to the life of others, by means of love, friendship, indignation, compassion."

—Simone de Beauvoir

By looking for blessings, I open up the path for life to flow.

Make a list of three things you are grateful for from each of the following categories: your home, your family, your work, your health or body, and your neighborhood.

_____

_____

_____

_____

_____

_____

_____

_____

_____

_____

_____

_____

_____

_____

_____

_____

_____

_____

We've all heard the phrase "turn lemons into lemonade." How can that apply to a difficult situation you are going through right now? What are the lemons in your life? And what are the potential gifts and growth you may draw from those experiences?

_____

_____

_____

_____

_____

_____

_____

_____

_____

_____

_____

_____

_____

_____

_____

_____

A gentle and authentic smile can convey the feeling of gratitude without words. Notice times when you resist smiling and times when a smile comes easily. What is the difference between them? Brainstorm ways you can share your smile more often, adding joy to your own life and the lives of others.

_____

_____

_____

_____

_____

_____

_____

_____

_____

_____

_____

_____

_____

_____

_____

_____

"Feeling gratitude and not expressing it is like wrapping a present and not giving it."

—William Arthur Ward

Think of one of your favorite objects—something you can't imagine parting with. What about that object touches your heart? How can you share that thing (or the essence of it) with someone you love? Try writing a story or sharing its history and meaning to allow others to partake in your joy and know you better as well.

PRACTICE

Write a letter or email to a person who may feel lifted up by hearing how you feel. Tell them how much they mean to you and how you appreciate their love and kindness. You may choose to mail the letter or deliver it in person.

MEDITATION

This loving-kindness meditation will help you expand
your awareness, connection, and gratitude toward others.
Let your breath bring focus into your body and heart.
Close your eyes and envision someone whom you love
dearly. Imagine sending love and kindness to them and
honor the appreciation you feel for their presence in your
life. Breathe with that image in mind for a few breaths.

Now bring to mind someone with whom you have a
difficult relationship. See if you can send them loving-
kindness, too, wishing them peace, happiness, and health.
When you are finished, take a deep breath in and exhale
through your mouth. Come back into your awareness of
the room and your body, and gently open your eyes.

When you have an instinct to say "thanks," pause for a moment and see if you can expand on that word. When was the last time you just said "thanks" but meant so much more? Write out the authentic and full thank-you.

Taking good care of your personal possessions is a way to show appreciation for the things in your life. If there's something that you've neglected or that needs your attention—from a beloved shirt that has lost buttons to a car that needs maintenance—why did that happen? How can you be a better steward of your belongings in the future?

PRACTICE

Mindfulness and gratitude are great ways to enhance your spiritual connection during your daily life. Do you feel more at peace and centered when you slow down, become present, and acknowledge the gifts in your life? Write about one recent moment when you were mindful. How did that feel?

PRACTICE

Incorporate gratitude rituals into your daily life. At meals, you may say grace; after special times with friends, you may offer kind words for their time and friendship. Create a special code with lovers that reflects your appreciation, like a gentle squeeze on the arm or a wink. In return, allow others to participate in your gratitude.

I have everything I need.

Moments of gratitude don't have to be huge. Find something small in your life right now—a houseplant, a crayon, a paper clip—and write about how and why you appreciate it. How does it feel to see something so small and realize that it's a sign of the abundance of the world?

_____

_____

_____

_____

_____

_____

_____

_____

_____

_____

_____

_____

_____

_____

_____

_____

_____

Can you conjure a feeling of personal freedom? Perhaps you picture a summertime drive down a long country road at dusk, or time spent looking out at an ocean at sunset. What makes your spirit feel free and grateful to be alive?

Chapter Three
Give Back with Grace

Giving back with grace means giving without demand. The act of giving can open one's heart and create a greater sense of connection to your community and to the world at large. Personal contributions to the lives of others brings joy and fulfillment to your life, enhances your spiritual journey, and makes life a little easier for someone else. As you make an intentional and consistent choice to give, you expand your consciousness and create meaningful relationships with others whom you may not have otherwise met.

Extending acts of service can come in many forms. Some people have more time or energy than money, while others choose financial donations. There are plenty of ways to practice gracious giving, all with great impact. As you consider what you have to offer and the ways in which you'd like to give, remember that any contribution supports the collective growth of all.

"Somebody once said we never know what is enough until we know what's more than enough."

—Billie Holiday

Thinking about your local community, what is one thing that you often notice it needs? A volunteer to clean off the sidewalk by the senior citizen's center? A French/history/math expert who can help students with their homework at an after-school program? In what ways can you use your time, talent, or resources to make a small contribution to that need?

_____

_____

_____

_____

_____

_____

_____

_____

_____

_____

_____

_____

_____

_____

_____

PRACTICE

Clear out unused items from your closets, bathroom, and

pantry. Make a monthly practice of donating these items

to a women's shelter or girls' home in your area.

Think of something wonderful in your life that you may take for granted. What would it feel like to share that gift with others? Good? Eye-opening? Confusing? Write out some of the ways you could share this gift.

Connecting with your childlike heart gives you allowance to play, have fun, and feel free. Giving from this place might look like coaching youth sports or even offering encouragement to the athletes from the bleachers. What game or activity did you most enjoy as a child, and how can you support children now who enjoy that same activity?

_____

_____

_____

_____

_____

_____

_____

_____

_____

_____

_____

_____

_____

_____

_____

_____

My life is abundant, and I have plenty to offer.

Sometimes, we can offer something less tangible, such as a prayer, a peace offering, or even giving someone the benefit of the doubt. How can you be mindful in an intangible way and give graciously today?

_____

_____

_____

_____

_____

_____

_____

_____

_____

_____

_____

_____

_____

_____

_____

MEDITATION

Take a deep breath and close your eyes. Notice how you feel, physically and emotionally. Bring awareness to your thoughts and take a few breaths to acknowledge your state of being. When you begin to judge yourself, see if you can find acceptance. Give yourself time to be still and simply witness your life. As you extend compassion to yourself, you connect to your higher heart.

Now bring to mind a friend or loved one who might have said or done something hurtful to you in the past. See if you can expand your perspective and consciousness, making room for forgiveness and compassion. You may notice emotions begin to stir. Allow the emotions to be present as you breathe steadily. Take your time and when you feel ready, on the next inhale, gently open your eyes.

Feeling grace for others is a beautiful gift that begins in the heart. Is there a person in your life who is struggling with self-worth issues or constantly judging themselves? Do you know someone challenged with financial issues or learning difficulties? How could you extend extra kindness to them, or anyone else, today?

_____

_____

_____

_____

_____

_____

_____

_____

_____

_____

_____

_____

_____

_____

_____

Random acts of kindness are fun ways to give with grace. Pay for the gas or coffee for the person in line behind you. Leave an extra tip for a hardworking server. Leave your change behind on the counter at the market. Make a list of ways you can pay it forward. Doing so anonymously makes giving even more gracious!

_____

_____

_____

_____

_____

_____

_____

_____

_____

_____

_____

_____

_____

_____

_____

_____

_____

Small business owners always need a helping hand. Supporting entrepreneurs by donating your time, offering your services, or shopping locally will boost their businesses and help your community thrive. Which local entrepreneurs do you support? How do you support them? Can you increase that support at all?

_____

_____

_____

_____

_____

_____

_____

_____

_____

_____

_____

_____

_____

_____

Parents with young children are often in need of ideas, help, and encouragement. Think of the parents or grandparents you know who are caring for young children. What skills do you have that could be useful to them? Tutoring, reading, writing, arts and crafts, ridesharing, and cooking can be very helpful to offer overworked parents and caretakers. If you don't have a skill that feels like a match, you can still offer time or a basic service, like driving to pick up some of their dry cleaning.

PRACTICE

Cook a dinner or make a gift basket filled with practical items and leave it on the doorstep of someone you know who needs care. Or, make a stranger's day and drop it off on their doorstep anonymously!

MEDITATION

Close your eyes and bring your focus to your breath. Deepen your focus on the breath, without deepening the breath itself, and follow it as it flows into your chest.

As you inhale, imagine breathing in abundance. Inhale the life force and all of the resources the universe has gifted to you. As you exhale, imagine the breath flowing out through your heart, sending light, love, and resources back out into the world. This type of conscious breathing offers a continuous exchange of energy between you and the universe. As you breathe, allow your heart to open as you offer the breath of hope and peace to others.

After-school programs, senior centers, and places of worship always need to keep their programs funded, fresh, and engaging. Do you have skills such as fundraising, cooking, reading aloud, driving a van, teaching an exercise class, or writing that you can offer to such organizations?

_____

_____

_____

_____

_____

_____

_____

_____

_____

_____

_____

_____

_____

_____

_____

Consider things that you may need at some stage of life as you age or undergo medical treatment. Make a list of life-enhancing donations, such as hair, blood, organs, or time and consider which of these you may be able to gift now or prepare to gift in the future to those in need.

_____

_____

_____

_____

_____

_____

_____

_____

_____

_____

_____

_____

_____

_____

_____

_____

Reflect on your greatest passions. Do you share these passions with others? If not, write down a couple of ways you could introduce, teach, or simply enjoy your passion with a loved one soon. Even if they do not end up sharing your passion, they will enjoy getting to experience something meaningful to you and learning something new about you.

When I give to others,
peace, love, and joy are given to me.

Many people in the world experience loneliness. Some of that loneliness could be eliminated by a simple visit from a friend or stranger, a game of cards, or time spent knitting or sharing music with others. Do you have any skills or abilities you could share with people at a retirement or nursing home, or perhaps with a lonely neighbor? Sometimes, simply giving your time to chat will be enough to make a difference.

_____

_____

_____

_____

_____

_____

_____

_____

_____

_____

_____

_____

_____

_____

_____

When you tap into your heart, you may notice a particular area where you feel you have the most compassion to give. You may be called to support the sick or work with parents trying to adopt. Perhaps rescuing animals calls your heart. What types of groups or people do you feel most compassion for, and what needs of theirs might you be able to help with?

_____

_____

_____

_____

_____

_____

_____

_____

_____

_____

_____

_____

_____

_____

_____

_____

_____

Your creativity serves more than just your inner passions. Art, music, crafts, poetry, and household projects inspire others and bring renewed life. How can you share your creativity and spread its joy out into the world?

_____

_____

_____

_____

_____

_____

_____

_____

_____

_____

_____

_____

_____

_____

_____

_____

"You cannot hope to build a better world without improving the individuals. To that end each of us must work for his own improvement, and at the same time share a general responsibility for all humanity, our particular duty being to aid those to whom we think we can be most useful."

—Marie Curie

Many sacred texts discuss sharing food as an act of communion. While preparing food for yourself or your family, whom could you offer a meal to or share communion with? College students, neighbors who live alone, or people struggling with food scarcity issues may love a warm meal.

PRACTICE

Some children struggle to feel safe, encouraged, and validated. Some crave food, others companionship. Consider ways to support a child or group of children who may be struggling with basic needs in your community. Many organizations save lives with the help of volunteers or monetary donations. Extend your family by creating special bonds with children whom you may never physically meet.

MEDITATION

Uncross your arms and legs and leave your palms faceup on your lap. Bring your focus to your breath and breathe through your nostrils. Allow your mind to recall a time when you were very excited to give a present to a loved one. Feel their excitement and joy when they opened it. Expand this feeling by using the breath. Allow your whole body to vibrate with love and enthusiasm as you remember how you prepared the special gift or imagine giving them a new gift. Breathe that visualization into life and allow your body to benefit from the positive endorphins of love and joy.

Think about your local community garden or farmers' market. What needs do they have? List some ways you could become more involved, even if you don't have much free time.

_____

_____

_____

_____

_____

_____

_____

_____

_____

_____

_____

_____

_____

_____

_____

_____

_____

_____

Keeping your sidewalk and outdoor area clean may seem more like a responsibility than a joy, but it adds to the enjoyment and safety of others. How can you show your love and pride for your neighborhood by beautifying your space?

_____

_____

_____

_____

_____

_____

_____

_____

_____

_____

_____

_____

_____

_____

_____

_____

If you were to donate your time, would you like to work with children, teenagers, single parents, or the elderly? Brainstorm opportunities available at schools, churches, or nonprofit organizations and consider how much time you could offer each month.

_____

_____

_____

_____

_____

_____

_____

_____

_____

_____

_____

_____

_____

_____

_____

_____

PRACTICE

Many programs collect items such as used phones, electronics, or printer cartridges to recycle and use for fundraisers. Practice collecting your items each quarter and donating them to a program that you believe in.

The more I give from my heart,
the richer my life becomes.

Make a list of your local food shelters, churches, or community organizations that cook weekly meals for the underserved. Consider what kind of supplies they may need to fulfill their mission. If you don't know, it is okay to call and ask. Do you have extra supplies, such as canned goods, paper products, utensils, or fresh veggies that you could donate to one of these organizations?

_____

_____

_____

_____

_____

_____

_____

_____

_____

_____

_____

_____

_____

_____

_____

_____

Write a list of your professional skills. Often, people need legal counsel, healing services, accounting services, realty assistance, or even creative agencies to help them move forward in their lives, but they may not have the budget to hire someone for these services. What might you be able to offer as a pro bono service each month to someone who needs your skills?

_____

_____

_____

_____

_____

_____

_____

_____

_____

_____

_____

_____

_____

_____

_____

Chapter Four

Embody Compassion

Compassion is love in action: a feeling deep within that prompts us to act in hopes of alleviating someone else's suffering. As a spiritual act, when practiced intentionally, compassion expands your capacity for love and kindness as you care for the spirit and soul of another. As you grow in spiritual awareness, you gain greater insight and sensitivity to humanity, allowing you to better identify your own and other's pains and struggles.

Embodying compassion helps open your heart and reinforces empathy and forgiveness. Spiritual compassion offers grace and asks us to humbly participate in the well-being of one another. In order to have compassion for others, we must first have it for ourselves. In this chapter, we will focus on ways to become more vulnerable as we build authentic relationships. Through compassion, we foster connection, become inspired, and feel empowered as we seek to better our mental, physical, and spiritual lives.

Consider the ways you show compassion to others, especially young children who are hurting or scared. In what ways can you extend that same kind of compassion to yourself when you are hurting or scared?

_____

_____

_____

_____

_____

_____

_____

_____

_____

_____

_____

_____

_____

_____

_____

_____

PRACTICE

Practice compassion by going the extra mile and offering what you can to someone in need. Today, let that someone be you. Practice taking the time you need for self-care, quiet time, or rest. Reach out to others and ask for help or simply a listening ear.

Acknowledging the inner critic is the first step toward accepting the pains and insecurities you've experienced. Write about the ways you have accepted the shortcomings of others. Then make a list of your own perceived shortcomings or failures. What does it feel like to accept self-compassion for all you've been through?

_____

_____

_____

_____

_____

_____

_____

_____

_____

_____

_____

_____

_____

_____

_____

Compassion is an act that shows empathy and kindness. Make a list of the ways you are hard on yourself. Read the list from a third-person perspective. How would you show compassion to a friend if that list were theirs?

_____

_____

_____

_____

_____

_____

_____

_____

_____

_____

_____

_____

_____

_____

_____

_____

_____

I love myself exactly the way that I am.

A way to deepen your compassion for yourself and others is to learn to respond rather than react. What is a typical reaction you have when you feel afraid, triggered, or upset? Think of three other ways you could respond that involve using perspective and the ability to pause instead.

_____

_____

_____

_____

_____

_____

_____

_____

_____

_____

_____

_____

_____

_____

_____

_____

_____

_____

MEDITATION

Sit or lie down and allow yourself to fully relax. Bring your focus to your breath as it enters your nose. Become centered and still. Call to mind a time when you felt hurt or scared. Imagine viewing yourself at that time from an outside perspective. As you witness yourself in pain, imagine offering kindness and love to yourself. What does she need? How can you offer her comfort? Visualize wrapping your arms around that woman, telling her it will be okay and that you understand her pain. Tell her that you love her, you accept her, and you are here for her.

What connects you to everyone else? Make a list of the ways in which you feel connected to friends, family, and humanity. The ways in which we are similar are far greater than the ways we are different.

Being thoughtful and kind toward others will lift them up.
What types of compliments make you feel good? What kind
of compliments could you offer others in order to magnify
their strengths?

_____

_____

_____

_____

_____

_____

_____

_____

_____

_____

_____

_____

_____

_____

_____

_____

_____

_____

Pick one person you've known for a long time but don't know too much about. What would you like to ask them specifically about their career, their family, or their education? What insights into their lives might you gain from knowing these things about them?

_____

_____

_____

_____

_____

_____

_____

_____

_____

_____

_____

_____

_____

_____

_____

_____

_____

"The whole idea of compassion . . . is based on a keen awareness of the interdependence of all . . . living beings, which are all part of one another and all involved in one another."

—Thomas Merton

What are some small acts of kindness that you can share with a compassionate heart? Opening a door for someone, offering to carry their groceries, extending a hug, or offering simple words of encouragement go a long way to alleviate the burden someone else may carry. Make a list of kind acts that have been given to you, and ones you'd like to extend to others.

_____

_____

_____

_____

_____

_____

_____

_____

_____

_____

_____

_____

_____

_____

_____

_____

PRACTICE

Making a meaningful connection with a person is a way to show compassion. Maintaining good eye contact is an intimate way to let another person know that you see them and that you are listening because they matter. This vulnerable practice helps you to stay present in the moment and opens your heart more fully.

MEDITATION

Start by taking three long and deep breaths. Notice any

lingering thoughts and let them gently drift away with

the breath. Bring your awareness to your body, between

your throat and your lower abdomen. Breathing with

great attention, notice which emotions feel present. Is

there a tense grip of fear or unease in your stomach?

Is your heart brimming with anticipation? There is no

right or wrong answer; this meditation is simply about

becoming an observer. The more you can connect to your

own emotional body, the more you will be able to feel the

emotions of others. Let your body teach you and breathe

with the sensations.

The morning can be a time of reflection and intention setting for the day. A morning routine that includes affirmations, prayer, and gentle movement sets the tone of connection to one's self and others. Make a list of things you can do to create a 10- to 20-minute morning routine that includes kind and loving activities.

_____

_____

_____

_____

_____

_____

_____

_____

_____

_____

_____

_____

_____

_____

Fear can drive us to believe we are different, misunderstood, or superior to others. As we recognize and accept our own fear, we develop a more compassionate heart. We are more alike than we often realize. Which fears may be making you feel distant from others?

_____

_____

_____

_____

_____

_____

_____

_____

_____

_____

_____

_____

_____

_____

_____

_____

Validating the way someone feels, even if you don't fully understand it or agree with it, is a loving act of compassion. Choose one situation that you didn't fully understand or a person whose perspective you couldn't grasp. What could you have said to more fully acknowledge and honor this person's experience? What is a step you can take in future situations to validate the feelings of others?

_____

_____

_____

_____

_____

_____

_____

_____

_____

_____

_____

_____

_____

_____

In this moment, may I be kind to myself. May I give myself the compassion I need.

Acceptance doesn't necessarily mean that you agree with someone; it means that you respect their position or behavior as their own. List three new activities you could participate in to meet a more diverse group of people—like trying a new hobby or joining a local community organization. How would it feel to be out of your comfort zone? What fears arise? Is the idea exciting?

_____

_____

_____

_____

_____

_____

_____

_____

_____

_____

_____

_____

_____

_____

Increase patience with others when you feel aggravated or disappointed with their actions. Learn to pause, breathe, and remember that each person is working through struggles and weaknesses of their own. Who in your life could benefit from your patience this week?

Sometimes, we feel different than others or that our family cannot fully understand us. What are some common threads between you and a difficult family member that you can use to relate?

_____

_____

_____

_____

_____

_____

_____

_____

_____

_____

_____

_____

_____

_____

_____

_____

Supporting someone else's hopes and dreams can reinforce their belief in themselves and in life's possibilities. Is there someone you care for who has a dream and needs encouragement? Brainstorm two or three ways you could encourage them. They don't need to be big gestures—just deeply felt ones.

_____

_____

_____

_____

_____

_____

_____

_____

_____

_____

_____

_____

_____

_____

_____

_____

Staying in touch with the people who matter to you is a simple way to show compassion and kindness. Create a list of people whom you want to check in with each week. Call them, text them, or send them an email, letting them know you are thinking of them and offering your care should they need it.

MEDITATION

Start by closing your eyes or softly gazing at a lit candle or other soothing visual. Bring to mind someone whom you love, perhaps saying their name or visualizing them with you to bring their energy and essence into your awareness. Choose a phrase to repeat with your breath as an offering of compassion. Common phrases include "May you be happy and healthy" and "May you be free of suffering and pain." You may choose other people, your family as a group, or your community at large. You can also visualize yourself and repeat the phrase as an extension of love.

Accepting disagreements and other people's opinions that differ from your own is a loving way to honor another person. Compassion holds space for people to find their own way. Is there a person in your life with whom you disagree? In what ways can you validate their position and values?

_____

_____

_____

_____

_____

_____

_____

_____

_____

_____

_____

_____

_____

_____

_____

_____

_____

_____

Listening is a special act of compassion that needs practice and intention. Some people just want to be heard. Write about a time when someone was able to sit and listen to you without judgment or feedback. How did that make you feel? In what way can you become a better listener?

_____

_____

_____

_____

_____

_____

_____

_____

_____

_____

_____

_____

_____

_____

_____

_____

When you are with others, being fully present is an act of care and consideration. Write about the challenges you experience in giving someone your undivided attention. Does your phone distract you? Do you have a fear of intimacy or are your own thoughts requiring your attention? Is there a step you can take to better cope with one of these challenges?

_____

_____

_____

_____

_____

_____

_____

_____

_____

_____

_____

_____

_____

_____

_____

_____

"The best and most beautiful things in the world cannot be seen nor even touched, but just felt in the heart."

—Helen Keller

PRACTICE

This week, adopt a conscious practice of smiling. Offering

a smile can make others feel at ease and may brighten their

day. Smiling as a self-love practice can alleviate stress,

strengthen your immune system, and elevate your mood.

Smiling is contagious and an easy way to spread kindness.

Sometimes it is better to be kind than to be right. Today, I will practice kindness.

Empathy is a valuable spiritual act, one that allows your heart to expand and offers a deeper understanding to humanity. Imagine putting yourself in someone else's shoes. Write about a friend who may be going through a challenging situation. What might your experience be like if you were in their position?

_____

_____

_____

_____

_____

_____

_____

_____

_____

_____

_____

_____

_____

_____

_____

_____

_____

_____

_____

_____

Sharing someone else's joys and accomplishments is a heart connection that celebrates their triumphs and growth. It also encourages you to be the best version of yourself. Write about the joys you feel when watching your loved ones succeed.

Chapter Five
Embrace Your Highest Self

Your highest self, or true self, is the evolved being who lives within you. This is a wise and unconditionally loving aspect of you, connected to the Divine source and consciousness. Part of the spiritual journey is learning to embrace and sustain the connection to your highest self in your daily life. Although you may often be challenged with setbacks, if you keep an open heart, you can learn to use these trials to welcome expansion and growth. Taking the insights and meditations beyond this journal will give you the support that you need.

In this chapter, you will be guided to connect with you higher self by listening to your heart and intuition, sensing the call of your soul, and honoring that call with intentional living. You are an unlimited being, full of possibility, wisdom, and wonder. As you connect more deeply within, you connect more deeply with the world, creating a legacy that leaves an impression of compassion, love, and peace.

It takes courage to open your heart. Notice the times when you feel imperfect, flawed, or self-conscious. Counter that by remembering your worth. Write about the ways that you are lovable and worthy, listing your qualities of strength and character and your unique gifts.

_____

_____

_____

_____

_____

_____

_____

_____

_____

_____

_____

_____

_____

_____

_____

_____

PRACTICE

Using your intuition can help you embrace your higher
wisdom and connect you to the natural flow of the
universe. Before making decisions—even if they are
routine choices—practice pausing and listening to the
voice of your higher self before acting on your intuition.
The more you practice, the more you will learn to discern
between your mind and your intuitive guidance.

Think about all of the women you admire. Write out a list of each woman's characteristics that you most admire or love— their confidence, kindness, or sense of humor. When you're done writing, put the words "I AM" in front of each characteristic on the list.

_____

_____

_____

_____

_____

_____

_____

_____

_____

_____

_____

_____

_____

_____

_____

_____

_____

_____

_____

_____

You have a certain energy depending on your mood, recent experiences, past wounds, and sense of self. Other people also have their own energy, which sometimes causes us frustration or judgment. Who in your life is difficult to be around? Write about that relationship, reflecting on their energy and how it differs from yours. Are there steps you can take to make dealing with their energy feel less frustrating?

I bow to infinite intelligence
and creative wisdom. I bow to the
Divine teacher within.

Providing your physical body with optimal nutrition improves health, elevates mood, increases stamina, and raises your overall vibration. Write a list of the ideal foods, nutrients, and supplements you know your body needs in order to feel lighter and more vibrant. Then list the less nutritious items you can release from your diet.

_____

_____

_____

_____

_____

_____

_____

_____

_____

_____

_____

_____

_____

_____

_____

_____

MEDITATION

Close your eyes and breathe simply and slowly as you allow your body to relax more deeply with each exhale. Gently bring to mind a memory in which you have feelings of guilt or remorse. Notice the reaction of judgment and discomfort that may arise and just breathe.

On your next inhalation, imagine being lifted by a cloud and moving through the sky. With each cycle of breath, visualize moving through the air on the cloud, and releasing judgments of your past, feelings of unease, and negative self-beliefs. As you continue to release, the cloud becomes even lighter. When you feel complete, use your exhaling breath to bring your cloud back down to the ground. Observe your breath entering into the body and become present in the moment. Gently open your eyes.

Prayer, rituals, and meditation can help us stay connected to our higher selves. Who or what do you call upon for guidance and support? Angels, personal guides, animal totems, ancestors, and Sacred Spirit are all available as part of your soul tribe. Write about those you feel connected to and what the relationships mean to you.

Spending time in nature helps ground your energy, mind, and body. Forest bathing and spending time near natural water sources can help relieve stress, improve sleep, assist in releasing emotional trauma, and improve your immunity. Where is your favorite outdoor location and how does it feed your soul? How can you make time to get there more often?

_____

_____

_____

_____

_____

_____

_____

_____

_____

_____

_____

_____

_____

_____

_____

Notice the motivations behind your activities and choices in your life. Are you motivated by fear, guilt, or love? Create a two-column list. On the left side, note your activities and obligations. On the right, note the energy or emotion you bring to each activity. Reflect on ways you can reframe your thinking and become more motivated by love.

"Do one thing every day that scares you."

—Mary Schmich

Make a list of your perceived failures or mistakes, indicating the approximate date when each one occurred. Beside each one, write something that you learned from the experience.

_____

_____

_____

_____

_____

_____

_____

_____

_____

_____

_____

_____

_____

_____

_____

_____

_____

_____

PRACTICE

Sacred ceremonies and rituals are ways to reconnect with your higher self and with Divine nature. Using oils, sage smudging, sound, crystals, and herbs can help keep you and your environment clear, cleansed, and vibrating at a higher level. Develop a monthly or seasonal ritual or ceremony to help your spirit soar. A new moon blessing or equinox ceremony can help usher in the callings of your heart.

MEDITATION

Let yourself relax with a soft gaze. Recall times when you have been hurt or experienced trauma. Though it can be tempting to deny your emotions in difficult times, breathe in and out with the difficult feelings and allow yourself to just be.

Take one breath in, repeating the mantra "I accept the way I feel right now. I accept this moment." Let your breath guide you to the inner dialogue that says, "I feel this, and although it's uncomfortable, I accept what I've experienced." When you find acceptance, you acknowledge the impact of your truth. There's no separation from self and reality; instead, there is a connection of presence, awareness, and understanding. When you are ready, take a deep breath and come back to the moment.

Being present helps eliminate anxieties by keeping your focus on the current reality. Take time to observe this moment, and then list five to ten things that you notice using your senses of sight, sound, taste, touch, and smell. Engage your emotional senses, and write what you see and feel in this moment.

_____

_____

_____

_____

_____

_____

_____

_____

_____

_____

_____

_____

_____

_____

_____

_____

_____

Personal growth and mindfulness help us become more aware of when we've made decisions based on other people's opinions or based on our own desires for our lives. What choices do you need to start making for yourself? Write about how you can choose to create a life that is happy and healing for you.

_____

_____

_____

_____

_____

_____

_____

_____

_____

_____

_____

_____

_____

_____

Think about decisions or actions that you have been putting off or procrastinating on instead of accomplishing. Write out two different options of how to move forward. They can be drastically different or diverge only slightly—write whatever feels right. Let yourself sit with the words and tune into how you feel with each option on the page. Circle the decision that feels most aligned with your heart.

_____

_____

_____

_____

_____

_____

_____

_____

_____

_____

_____

_____

_____

_____

_____

_____

Even though I may feel
anxious or unsure,
I deeply and completely love
and accept myself.

What are some of the most uncomfortable emotions for you to feel? Which emotions do you need to learn to process more fully? Write these emotions down and reflect on what the emotions are trying to teach you. What can you learn from your discomfort?

_____

_____

_____

_____

_____

_____

_____

_____

_____

_____

_____

_____

_____

_____

_____

_____

When you create healthy boundaries, you create a safe zone within which you can operate. Healthy boundaries don't push people away. In fact, boundaries help deepen trust and intimacy with others. Make a list of the boundaries you currently have in place with loved ones, coworkers, and other people who make a positive or negative impact on your life. Add to the list the boundaries your higher self is asking you to enforce. You may need to write one list for family, another for friends, and others for volunteer organizations or work.

Learning the language of your intuition will help you trust your deep well of inner wisdom. Write about a time when you had clear intuition and followed its guidance, noting the experience that followed. Then write about a time when you didn't follow your intuition. How can you learn to listen to your intuition more often?

_____

_____

_____

_____

_____

_____

_____

_____

_____

_____

_____

_____

_____

_____

_____

_____

Some days are harder than others. Sitting with what is difficult and growing comfortable in the discomfort is one way to strengthen and heal. Write out what is difficult for you this week, then read that aloud from a third-person perspective. How would you offer comfort if this were a friend's experience?

_____

_____

_____

_____

_____

_____

_____

_____

_____

_____

_____

_____

_____

_____

_____

_____

PRACTICE

Movement as meditation helps connect the breath with intention and creates space and flow in the body. Consider adding a new yoga, tai chi, or qigong practice into your life to increase health while also focusing on your spiritual awakening.

MEDITATION

Close your eyes and use your breath to go deep within.
Then take three deep breaths to let your body know that
it is time to relax. On your next inhale, visualize stepping
into a hot air balloon. As you breathe in, the balloon
begins to lift into the air.

Each inhalation helps the balloon rise, and each
exhalation allows you to observe more of the environment.
As you ascend, you are able to see the rooftops; as your
perspective widens, you can see the entire city. Take a
moment to pause and look around. Feel the air. Allow your
worries to remain down on the ground becoming smaller in
size and threat. As you rise up, feel connected to an energy
that is much larger than you are. With awe, appreciation,
and a higher perspective, notice the lightness and freedom
in your heart. Stay here as long as you'd like.

Authenticity takes courage and vulnerability. The more you build self-confidence, the more you can shine your light and share it with the world. What insecurities are you holding on to that have caused you to hide parts of yourself? Who is a safe person who you can reveal your true self to without fear?

_____

_____

_____

_____

_____

_____

_____

_____

_____

_____

_____

_____

_____

_____

_____

_____

_____

As you embrace change, you signal to a higher power that you trust in the timing and plan designed for your life. What changes are you resisting, and how can you become more open to new possibilities?

_____

_____

_____

_____

_____

_____

_____

_____

_____

_____

_____

_____

_____

_____

_____

_____

_____

Learning to listen to your higher self can start with simple communication. Start a dialogue by writing down some of your concerns and asking your higher self for guidance with these particular situations. Take a moment to listen and write what you hear.

_____

_____

_____

_____

_____

_____

_____

_____

_____

_____

_____

_____

_____

_____

_____

_____

"If you do not tell the truth about yourself you cannot tell it about other people."

—Virginia Woolf

MEDITATION

Meditation doesn't have to be a planned event. You can meditate in any moment, for however long you'd like, in any place that feels right—a park on your lunch break, a commuter train, a waiting room. Practice taking short breaks during the day to re-center yourself by bringing your focus to the moment, using your breath or an external object to focus your awareness. Use a mantra or a simple thought, like "I am breathing, I am here," to shift from the chaos of the world to internal peace.

I am worthy of love, peace, and abundance. I am abundant.

Recognize the beauty in all things. Even the places and things we often overlook have a certain character to them and are beautiful in their own way. Where do you see beauty in the world? Write about the beauty you see in your home, in nature, with loved ones, and in yourself. Try to think of one thing you generally overlook and write about its character and beauty.

_____

_____

_____

_____

_____

_____

_____

_____

_____

_____

_____

_____

_____

_____

There is a reason for every experience that occurs in your life. Some experiences feel wonderful and some are difficult. Write down a challenging experience you've had, along with the insights and wisdom you gained. Reflect on the potential reasons these experiences found you, and how you've grown to appreciate each one.

_____

_____

_____

_____

_____

_____

_____

_____

_____

_____

_____

_____

_____

_____

_____

_____

Resources

Websites

Avaiya.Com
DailyOm.Com
Gaia.Com
LeahGuy.Com
MantraMag.Com
PsychologyToday.Com
TheShiftNetwork.Com
YogaJournal.Com

Books

Guy, Leah. *The Fearless Path: A Radical Awakening to Emotional Healing and Inner Peace.* Newburyport, Massachusetts: Weiser, 2017.

Guy, Leah. *Overcoming Toxic Emotions: A Practical Guide to Building Better Relationships with Yourself and Others.* New York: Skyhorse, 2021.

References

Chödrön, Pema. *Start Where You Are: A Guide to Compassionate Living*. Boulder, CO: Shambhala, 2018.

Curie, Marie. *Pierre Curie with Autobiographical Notes*. Translated by Charlotte and Vernon Kellogg. New York: Macmillan, 1923.

de Beauvoir, Simone. "De Beauvoir on the crusher of men" (excerpt from *Old Age*). *The Guardian* March 14, 1972. https://www.theguardian.com/news/1972/mar/15/mainsection.fromthearchive

Holiday, Billie. "Lady Sings the Blues." Goodreads. Accessed on November 11, 2020. https://www.goodreads.com/work/quotes/1111829-lady-sings-the-blues

Keller, Helen. *The Story of My Life*. New York: Dover Publications, 1996.

Merton, Thomas. Qtd. in JoEllen Goertz Koerner, RN, PhD, FAAN, *Healing Presence: The Essence of Nursing*. Springer Publishing Company, 2007.

Nin, Anaïs. *The Diary of Anaïs Nin*. Vol. 1: 1931–1934. New York: Houghton Mifflin Harcourt, 1969.

Schmich, Mary. https://quoteinvestigator.com/2013/08/09/scare/

Shelley, Mary Wollstonecraft. Quotes.net, STANDS4 LLC, 2020. "Mary Wollstonecraft Shelley Quotes."Accessed November 11, 2020. https://www.quotes.net/quote/17479.

Stanton, Elizabeth Cady. Qtd. in Carol Gilligan. *In a Different Voice*. Cambridge, MA: Harvard University Press, 2009.

Ward, Willliam Arthur. *Thoughts of a Christian Optimist*. Droke House Press, 1968.

Woolf, Virginia. 1974. "The Moment and Other Essays." https://quotecatalog.com/quote/virginia-woolf-if-you-do-not-t-8ab282a.

Acknowledgments

With a humble and grateful heart, I would like to thank the people who have supported me on my personal journey and in my work. This book would not have been possible without the fine editors at Callisto Media, in particular Susan Haynes and Lia Ottaviano, for believing that I was the right person to birth this special project.

For the amazing teachers, healers, friends, partners, and opportunities over the years—all of whom have helped me grow spiritually, mentally, and emotionally—I am grateful. It is my connection to each of them that has encouraged my bravery to take risks in order to live a full and meaningful life. I have deep appreciation for all of the clients who have confided in me and entrusted part of their emotional and spiritual healing to my hands. It has been an honor to be part of their process and watch them blossom.

The following women are friends who have become family and hold a special place in my heart: Helen Rodgers, Cindy Chase, Laura Zaccardi, Rainer Montgomery, Joan Palmer, Marilys Ernst, Colleen Canyon, and Abby Weidel.

I am grateful for Cheryl King and Rick Guy, whom I've been blessed to have as parents, and all of my family who have taught me about life and love. For the grace that is constantly bestowed upon me by God, and for the compassion given to me by others, I am so grateful. Thank you.

About the Author

Leah Guy is an intuitive spiritual healer, mindfulness expert, and author of *The Fearless Path: A Radical Awakening to Emotional Healing and Inner Peace* and *Overcoming Toxic Emotions: A Practical Guide to Building Better Relationships with Yourself and Others*. She combines professional training with her personal triumphs over abuse, addiction, and anxiety to help others heal, address emotional wounds and limited beliefs, and access their fullest potential.

A sought-after inspirational speaker and retreat facilitator, Leah has appeared on top media outlets as an expert on mind-body connection, energy medicine, and emotional and spiritual healing. She has a BA in communications, a CMT from the Alive & Well! Institute of Conscious Bodywork, and studied at The School of Enlightenment and Healing. Leah maintains a private practice in the New York City metro area. For more information, visit LeahGuy.com and follow her on social @leahguylive.